I0164973

A Light unto my Path

by Eliza Wright

ISBN: 978-1-78364-431-5

www.obt.org.uk

Unless indicated otherwise Scripture quotations are taken from the Holy Bible, New International Version Anglicised Copyright © 1979, 1984, 2011 Biblica. Used by permission of Hodder & Stoughton Ltd, an Hachette UK company. All rights reserved. 'NIV' is a registered trademark of Biblica UK trademark number 1448790.

****

The Open Bible Trust

Fordland Mount, Upper Basildon,

Reading, RG8 8LU, UK.

A Light to my Path

Contents

Page

A Light unto my Path

An Introduction to

'Rightly Dividing the Word of Truth.'

2 Timothy 2:15
(King James Authorised Version.)

Introduction

Introduction ...

There's a maze on the front cover of this booklet. Not just the one path but a whole tangle of them, and you might well ask, why? What does it mean? Well, for a start there's a link between the maze and the Bible. Many people find the Bible to be a bit of a maze and right division shows us a path through it, but before we get on to that, I think we ought to consider briefly a couple of other points.

Obviously I've no idea how familiar each reader is with the Christian Bible. Many people have a basic knowledge, and at least know the Old Testament from the New. Many also believe it's the Word of God. That's a good start, but the word 'start' implies future progress. I believe that as Christians, part of our role is to understand Scripture to the best of our ability, and to move forward in our knowledge and faith, not only for our own sake, but also to help others. To this end, right division is the best navigation device I've ever come across.

The next thing I want to do is to set out the parameters within which my argument rests. The things I regard as non-negotiable, the things I'd call 'constants' if I were conducting a scientific inquiry. I'll begin with my absolute conviction that our Lord and Saviour Jesus Christ is the Son of God. His appearance on earth, His sacrifice by death on the cross, and His subsequent resurrection, are totally fundamental aspects of my faith.

Another important point to make is that 'right division' does not mean selecting the parts of scripture we happen to like, and discarding the rest. The term 'right division' comes from the Apostle Paul's second letter to Timothy, in the *King James Authorised Version*:

> Study to shew thyself approved unto God, a workman that needeth not to be ashamed, *rightly dividing* the word of truth. (2 Timothy 2:15; *KJV*)

So what did Paul mean? Well, put simply, it means dividing up the Word of God so that we have some idea which parts apply to *us*, *now*, and which do not.

Okay!
Back
to the maze!

Okay!
Back to the maze!

At the bottom of the picture is a quote from the Old Testament Book of Proverbs (3:6; *KJV*). It says that if you trust in the Lord he will *direct* your paths. Now the word for 'direct' in the Greek translation of the Old Testament, with which Paul would have been very familiar, is the same word that the Apostle uses when he tells us to *rightly divide* the word of truth in the New. Could this be a hint that we're going in the right direction?

I believe that if God is pleased to guide our lives, He's also prepared to help us out with the road map of His book. He has, let's face it, a big advantage over us when it comes to choosing the right path. He has foreknowledge. He knows what's going to happen next. He can see the big picture. Just as we can look down on the maze on the front cover, and see our way through from one side to the other without too much trouble.

Unfortunately, we seldom have such a clear view, either in our lives or when we first begin seriously to study the Bible. Instead, it can be more like being dropped in a maze in the middle of the night! Day dawns, but we find the hedges are way above our head. We come to a fork in the road, and there's no sign post. Now and again we discover a place that seems vaguely familiar, but mostly we plod on bewildered, and in that state it's all too easy, in life as well as in Scripture, to set off in the wrong direction or follow the wrong guide.

Are you lost when it comes to making sense of the Bible? Are you going round in circles? Unsure which way to go next, who to follow and what to believe? Help may be at hand. Read on!

If you've never come across the idea of right division before, don't be too surprised. You're not alone. Many people who consider themselves Christians will look blank and say, 'What on earth is that? Never heard of such a thing!'

The Bible was written by many different writers over a long period of time, and is directed towards many different kinds of people; Jews, Gentiles, believers and unbelievers. Its division would seem to be common sense. The big questions are how and where do we divide it? And what are we to do with the result?

It amazes me that so many people are satisfied with a Bible that seems to contradict itself about several fundamental questions. People who are otherwise committed Christians are apparently content to treat the Bible as a random collection of historical documents, myths and propaganda that just happen to have survived. These, they say, have combined to produce a text which cannot wholly be relied upon.

What such people are actually saying is that they are happy to trust, for their eternal salvation, in a God who can't even look after a book!

Can this be right?

I think not. I think if God has left us a collection of ancient manuscripts to decipher, He is also going to leave us a few clues to direct us. I think the solution is to use God's guidance, and to use His book.

So perhaps we should add another constant:

All scripture is inspired by God.

All scripture is inspired by God.

Which God tells us, via the Apostle Paul again, in 2 Timothy:

> All scripture *is* given by inspiration of God, and *is* profitable for doctrine, for reproof, for correction, for instruction in righteousness: (2 Timothy 3:16; *KJV*)

Because of this it's vital we study the Bible, all of it, but at the same time keeping in mind that *not* all of it is directly about us or for us. So what's the point of studying it all? The reason is that if you take Paul at his word (his *inspired* word) and you begin your study, you'll find that all scripture, from Genesis to Revelation, is inter-linked. Each part throws light on other parts. The detail of this is too large a subject to be dealt with here, and further reading is essential. The glossary and list of publications and sources at the end of the booklet will enable you to find out more.

So ...
back to
'right division'

So ... back to 'right division'

A brief word on terminology is appropriate here. Dividing the Scriptures produces a number of sections which apply to different people at different times. These sections are often referred to as 'dispensations'. To define the word more specifically, we can say that dispensations are different periods of administration in the Word of God, in which *different rules* apply. For this reason 'right division' is the key to 'dispensational truth'.

Now most Christians actually acknowledge a dispensational divide already, and don't realise it. Just try asking them what they are planning to sacrifice, a bullock or a lamb, or maybe a couple of turtle doves? They will probably react as if you've suggested something quite bizarre, yet these are clear commandments from the Old Testament, and there are dozens of others besides!

Others might say, 'But we don't have to do those things today; we don't live in Old Testament times. The sacrifice of Our Lord Jesus Christ has made all those old sacrifices obsolete!'

Good! If you can agree with that then right division has begun – at least partly. You can accept that there are different periods of administration in the Word of God in which *different rules* are in force.

As we said earlier, these periods are sometimes called dispensations. I believe that if we're to be obedient to the Word of God, we must try to find out which dispensation – or dispensations – are relevant for Christians *today,* and what rules apply. This is a big topic, and Christians hold many and varied opinions. To cover it all would be impossible in such a small space, so I intend to home in on just one aspect for now. I'm asking the fundamental question: *when* did the dispensation that applies to the time we live in start? Exactly what rules apply to us is a very important factor, but I'm leaving that for another day.

To begin very simply, I hope you'll agree that most of the Old Testament was written for and about the Jews, (also called the Children of Israel, the Israelites, or the Hebrews). Their obligations and observances no longer apply to us. We are living in 'New Testament Times'.

So does that mean ... The current dispensation begins with The New Testament?

So does that mean ... The current dispensation begins with The New Testament?

A good question! We say we're living in New Testament times, but *can* we actually date the beginning of the present dispensational period from the beginning of the New Testament, the start of the Lord's earthly ministry? Well, let's look at the Gospels and see what we find.

Consider Matthew 5. This may be familiar as the Sermon on the Mount. 'Blessed are the meek,' says the Lord Jesus, 'for they shall *inherit the earth*.' How many Christians today, I wonder, are expecting, through meekness, to inherit the earth and spend their eternal life there? However, in what appears to be a contradiction of that teaching, we are told in Ephesians 2:6-7 that we are seated in the heavenly realms and are going to spend coming ages there. And Colossians 3:2 tells us to set our affection on things above, not on things of the earth. There seems to be a difference in the teaching of the Sermon on the Mount and these letters.

Also in Matthew 5, our Lord has been speaking of keeping the Law of Moses, which all orthodox Jews were supposed to keep. He goes on:

> "Do not think that I have come to abolish the Law or the Prophets; I have not come to abolish them but to fulfill them. I tell you the truth, until heaven and earth disappear, not the smallest letter, not the least stroke of a pen, will by any means disappear from the Law until everything is accomplished. Anyone who breaks one of the least of these commandments and teaches others to do the same will be called least in the kingdom of heaven, but whoever practices and teaches these commands will be called great in the

kingdom of heaven." (Matthew 5:17–
19)

Well, let's consider a simple example. One of the
'Ten Commandments', (Exodus 20:8), is to keep
the Sabbath, the seventh day, (Saturday), holy.
Yet Christian leaders have taught for years that
there is no need to keep the Sabbath on a Saturday,
but to keep it on a Sunday instead. One might ask
why, when in Colossians 2:16 we read:

> Therefore do not let anyone judge you
> by what you eat or drink, or with
> regard to a religious festival, a New
> Moon celebration or a Sabbath day.

Again, another teaching in the Sermon on the
Mount comes in Matthew 5:42:

> "Give to the one who asks you, and do
> not turn away from the one who wants
> to borrow from you."

Well, if it was generally known that Christian
people were carrying that out, we should soon

have nothing left but a loin cloth – and someone might even borrow that! No, we do not follow that command, and right division will show us why we should not.

More directly, we might consider Matthew 10:5,6. The Lord Jesus is sending his disciples out to preach and says: "Do not go among the Gentiles ... Go rather to the lost sheep of Israel." Also in Matthew 15:24, where He is confronted by a Canaanite woman begging for help, the Lord answered, "I was sent only to the lost sheep of Israel." (Note, however, because of her *faith*, the Lord helped her).

But after considering just these few things, doesn't it seem reasonable to conclude that in starting the present dispensation with the gospels, we are trying to observe instructions which do not belong to us? Jesus was ministering to the people of Israel (Romans 15:8), who were under the Law of Moses. We are Gentiles, and are not under the Mosaic Law.

All right then ... How about starting at the Crucifixion?

All right then ...
How about starting at the Crucifixion?

This dramatic event would seem to draw a fairly clear line across the Christian faith. Suppose, then, that the current dispensation starts at the crucifixion? What instructions are given after that?

In the last chapter of Matthew's Gospel the Lord is risen and is speaking to His disciples:

> "Therefore go and make disciples of all nations, baptizing them in the name of the Father and of the Son and of the Holy Spirit, and teaching them to obey everything I have commanded you. And surely I am with you always, to the very end of the age." (Matthew 28:19,20)

Now, most Christian organisations make some effort to carry that out up to a point, but what is meant by 'everything I have commanded you'? Surely that must include giving to anyone who asks, not doing any work on Saturday and the other things to which we have referred earlier!

Even more curious, at the end of Mark we have several verses which are sometimes left in and sometimes left out. The trouble is that Christian organisations do not know what to do with them.

> "And these signs will accompany those who believe: In my name they will drive out demons; they will speak in new tongues; they will pick up snakes with their hands; and when they drink deadly poison, it will not hurt them at all; they will place their hands on sick people, and they will get well." (Mark 16:17,18)

You see that is the difficulty. These signs *do not* follow those who believe today, but they did follow believers in the Acts period, the 30 or so years following Christ's crucifixion. If a Christian today were to drink 'deadly poison', or handle a poisonous snake with no protection other than faith, he or she would soon die – and probably too late discover the truth of right division! So perhaps we were wrong in considering the crucifixion as a suitable starting date for the current dispensation.

Well ...
Perhaps we can
say
it began at
Pentecost?

Well ... Perhaps we can say it began at Pentecost?

The next great event is the feast of Pentecost described at the beginning of the Acts of the Apostles. Ah! Most Christians will say, 'That's it! That is the start of the present dispensation. When the Holy Spirit came down as He did in Acts 2, that was the start of the church, the church of the dispensation that applies to us today!'

Again, let's look into The Book. The scene is Jerusalem, which is significant to start with. Peter addresses the crowd as 'Men of Israel' (Acts 2:22). He doesn't mention Gentiles. Peter then goes on to quote Psalm 16 (Acts 2:25-28). What would the Gentiles of that day know of Psalm 16?

So who were those 'Parthians and Medes and residents of Mesopotamia' (Acts 2:9-11) to whom Peter was speaking? They were Jews, and converts to Judaism called proselytes. It says so in

Acts 2:11. Jerusalem would be full of such people because of the feast of Pentecost, a Jewish feast described in the Law of Moses. Peter had no idea that Pentecost might be the beginning of a new dispensation, he was still addressing only the Jews. The very people who had rejected and crucified their Messiah! Marvellous as it may seem, God was giving Israel another chance.

Look at the parable of the Fig Tree (Luke 13:6-10). For three years it bore no fruit and the owner wanted to cut it down. But the gardener said, give it another chance. Bearing in mind that parables often foreshadow God's plans, what do you make of it? During the three years of the Lord's ministry the fig tree (which represents Israel as a nation) bore no fruit. Our Lord's prayer on the cross was "Father forgive them for they do not know what they are doing." His plea, like that of the gardener responsible for the fig tree, was 'give it one more chance.' At Pentecost that chance came: Peter and the other Apostles 'dug around and fertilized' from that point right through the period covered by the Acts. The felling of the tree was postponed, but in the end it had to come.

Before we get there however, we must consider further the story of the Acts. At Pentecost, Peter explains the unusual happenings that were going on:

> "... this is what was spoken by the prophet Joel ... I will show wonders in the heaven above and signs on the earth below, blood and fire and billows of smoke. The sun will be turned to darkness and the moon to blood before the coming of the great and glorious day of the Lord." (Acts 2:16,19,20).

These strange words are not unique in the Scriptures for they also occur in Matthew 24:29,30 and they come again in the book of Revelation. What they are referring to are the tremendous happenings which are to take place at the Second Coming of our Lord, and this is what Peter was expecting. It was Israel's second chance, and so he says:

> "Repent, then, and turn to God ... and that he may send (again) the Christ,

who has been appointed for you—even Jesus." (Acts 3:19,20)

All these dramatic happenings would have been possible then, if only the Jews had repented. Many encouraging signs *were* given. They were speaking with tongues and healing the sick. 'And many wonders and miraculous signs were done by the apostles' (Acts 2:43, fulfilling Mark 16:17,18).

Also, a new society of Jews with a new constitution was formed:

> All the believers were together and had everything in common. Selling their possessions and goods, they gave to anyone as he had need. (Acts 2:44,45).

So *those* were the days when they could 'give to the one who asks you' and signs followed those who believed. Such things will probably be possible again at the Second Coming of the Lord. All those momentous events were just preliminary foreshadows of that great day. So you see, the church of the present dispensation could not possibly have begun at Pentecost. We must move further on still to the next possibility which is...

How about ... with Peter's visit to Cornelius?

How about ... with Peter's visit to Cornelius?

Cornelius and his friends were God-fearing Gentiles (Acts 10:2). Cornelius was not a proselyte, a convert to Judaism, but a God-fearer. These were Gentiles who attended the synagogue but who had not been circumcised.

When Peter was summoned to speak with them he was staggered. You can see the magnitude of his amazement by reading Acts 10:28. If Peter had not had the vision recorded in verses 11- 17 he would never have gone to visit Cornelius.

It just shows how the Jewish people had grown to consider the Lord as their national monopoly. Instead of which, God's design was to use the Jew to proclaim His grace and salvation throughout the world, a purpose He had declared to Abraham centuries before (Genesis 12:1-3). Peter, who was given the 'keys of the kingdom of heaven'

(Matthew 16:19) was driven at last to open the door to the Gentiles.

Was this then the beginning of the church of the current dispensation? No! These Gentiles were about to share in Israel's blessing. As Paul wrote later, they 'now share in the nourishing sap from the olive root' (Romans 11:17). The Jews were still God's people, and Paul used this tree allegory, that of the cultivated olive, to represent them.

The Gentiles were considered as a 'wild olive shoot'. They were to be grafted in to the fruitless, cultivated Jewish Olive, in order to jolt that tree into producing fruit, (Romans 11:11-14). (An interesting aside is that this practice was actually used in olive cultivation.)

It seems, then, that we must draw on a bit further. After the story of Cornelius, we find that Peter drops out of the picture, and the main character on the scene is the Apostle Paul.

So ...
Does the present dispensation begin with Paul's ministry?

So ... Does the present dispensation begin with Paul's ministry?

Significantly, Paul begins at Antioch (Acts 11:26), and not Jerusalem. The centre has moved out. Then he goes on several missionary journeys even further afield. However, we notice that wherever he goes he always goes first to the Jewish synagogue (e.g. Acts 13:5,14; 14:1; 17:1,2.) It is still the Jew first, and through the Jews to the Gentiles.

But there's a difference. These Gentiles did not have to become proselytes. They were not circumcised and Paul did not insist that they should be, or carry out any of the other rites and ceremonies concerned with the Law of Moses. To clarify this matter, Paul goes up to Jerusalem to tell his doctrine to James and the other apostles (Acts 15). The result of this visit is a double code of instructions: one for Jews, one for Gentiles. The Jews are to continue to obey the Law of Moses. But the Gentiles are given a much less rigorous regime: 'telling them to abstain from food polluted by idols, from sexual immorality, from the meat of strangled animals and from blood' (Acts 15:20).

Is this then ... the start of the present dispensation?

Is this then ... the start of the present dispensation?

Actually no! Not yet. There is no double code today. We don't have two sets of instructions, one for Jews and one for Gentiles. Like a wild graft in to a cultivated olive tree, the effect of that great influx of Gentile believers might have gone either way. It could have stirred the Jews to think again about their position and accept Christ, or they could have become even more obstinate and spurned their Messiah with hatred. This was their last chance – and sadly instead of taking it they dug in their heels and said 'No way!'

Next, look at Chapter 19. It brings us to Ephesus. Here we read that for three months Paul continued to speak boldly in the synagogue, but the apostle's doctrine was publicly denigrated by some of the Jews. As a result, Paul broke away from them and set up the Christian church at Ephesus, which became a distinct and separate body.

Now, in chapter 20 a great break takes place. Paul (an orthodox Jew still) wants to be at Jerusalem for the Feast of Pentecost (verse 16). It is a strikingly sad and sorrowful passage (verses 16-38). Paul knows that 'prison and hardships' are awaiting him at Jerusalem, but that doesn't shake his resolve to go. His friends and colleagues are distraught, they weep and hug him and finally let him get on board the ship, 'what grieved them most was his statement that they would never see his face again.' (Acts 20:38)

Later on in that journey, when Paul and his travelling companions are staying in Caesarea, they are visited by a prophet who emphasises the dangers Paul is going to face in Jerusalem. Again everyone urges him not to go. But Paul replies:

> "Why are you weeping and breaking my heart? I am ready not only to be bound, but also to die in Jerusalem for the name of the Lord Jesus." (Acts 21:13)

So what happened to Paul in Jerusalem? Well, he certainly had an exciting time, (and you can read about it in Acts 21:17 – 23:32), but he wasn't destined to die there. The stumbling block for the orthodox Jews turned out to be the fact that Paul was a Roman citizen. Although the Jewish High Priest tried to talk the Roman governor of Judea, Porcius Festus, into a plot to ambush Paul and kill him, Festus instead allowed Paul to appeal to Caesar and be judged in Rome (Acts 25:11).

Now Rome was the great centre of the world in those days, and the last outpost of organised Judaism. All that happened there we are told in 16 verses (Acts 28:16 - 31). Note that Paul is being kept under house-arrest at this point. He's chained to a Roman soldier, but is allowed to receive visitors and continue his ministry. He's still speaking to the Jews first, but even so the majority of them will not accept the Lord Jesus as their Messiah. Finally, in verse 26, Paul quotes the prophet Isaiah:

> "'You will be ever hearing but never understanding; you will be ever seeing

but never perceiving." For this people's heart has become calloused; they hardly hear with their ears, and they have closed their eyes. Otherwise they might see with their eyes, hear with their ears, understand with their hearts and turn, and I would heal them." (Acts 28:26-27)

He follows this up with:

"Therefore I want you to know that God's salvation has been sent to the Gentiles, and they will listen!" (Acts 28:28)

And that is what we've been waiting for. The olive tree of Israel is now cut down. From this point, for close on 2000 years God has had no dealings with the Jews *as a nation*. They have been scattered all over the world, as He said they would be (Deuteronomy 32:26).

So what next? Well, the door is now wide open. To Paul has been entrusted a further message, of which he writes in the epistles to the Ephesians, Philippians and Colossians, and you may like to read these.

In Ephesians he tells us that in former times God singled the Jews out as being special. The Gentiles, more or less anybody else in the world who was not a Jew, were like aliens and strangers from God. But now, because of Christ's work and His sacrifice on the cross, and the Jewish failure to recognise this, the Gentiles were to be allowed to approach God directly.

So, no longer has the Jew a favoured place. No longer do the Gentiles depend on the Jewish nation for their knowledge of God. They, as Gentiles, are 'brought near through the blood of Christ.' The door is open. The new dispensation has begun.

So what can we say about the blessings for this new era? Well, for a start we shall not find them in the Old Testament, or in the Acts of the Apostles, or in any of the epistles written before the end of Acts. For them, and also special promises which were not mentioned before, we must search through the letters Paul wrote after the end of Acts: Ephesians, Colossians and Philippians, 1 and 2 Timothy, Titus and Philemon. And when we've taken in all that, we'll have as much as we can manage without trying to tune our lives to accord with the regulations of previous dispensations which do not apply to us.

Note this does not mean that *all* the rules and regulations of previous dispensations have been entirely abandoned and replaced by new ones. (The quotations from Proverbs and Psalms used on the front cover of this booklet are both from the Old Testament but are still valid, as are many of the moral regulations).

Nor does it mean that the Jews have now been rejected *en masse* by God, and their place taken over by Gentiles. The difference now, is that as far as God is concerned, we all have equal opportunity, whoever we are. Whoever our ancestors were, whatever we ourselves have done in the past, none of that makes any difference. All we need is Faith in Christ, which is sufficient for our salvation. As Paul says in Ephesians:

> For it is by **grace** you have been saved, through **faith**—and this not from yourselves, it is the **gift** of God. (Ephesians 2:8)

Conclusion

Conclusion

So, now that you've read a bit about right division what do you think?

If you don't know enough to make a decision, why not start learning? Don't just accept other peoples' opinions (not even mine!) but check it out for yourself. Discover the other hints and pointers that can help us to find our way.

I'm not claiming that this is a magic map, or that finding answers is always going to be easy. Now and then you're still going to find yourself on roads with illegible signposts. You're still going to ask questions that are hard to answer, questions no one else seems to have asked or found important, answers you have to work out for yourself.

One of those questions might be, shouldn't I be out there doing things instead of all this rather academic Bible study?

Well, should you? It's your decision. And yet...

Becoming a Christian, staying a Christian, are important decisions which will affect your whole life. Would you commit yourself to a lifelong job without – at the very least – reading the contract?

Conversely, if you've decided that Christ is not for you, is this really *your* conclusion? Or is it based on what other people have told you about God, about the Lord Jesus, about what they think the Bible says? Or on what some of the established Christian faiths have done in Christ's name?

Forget all that. Find out for yourself. Get a Bible and make some time to devote to it. And if it all seems a bit too daunting, remember that not only are we here to help if we can, but even the most isolated person has the pathway of prayer. Ask our Heavenly Father through the Lord Jesus Christ to help you understand. Then, and only then, let Him guide you towards what you are going to do about it!

Glossary

Glossary

This is brief and limited. I hope it will be of some help to any reader unfamiliar with the terminology used in the Christian Bible.

Church – although most readily understood these days as referring to a building, it can also be used as a collective term for a group of Christians. The latter definition is the one used here.

Dispensations – different periods of administration in the Word of God. In these different periods, different rules are in force. The original Greek word is *oikonomia*, which refers to the administration of a household or an estate. You can think of it as a 'stewardship'. We are in effect managers of God's estate, looking after it for Him, and, naturally, the steward's duties will vary according to the situation prevailing at the time.

Epistle – usually a kind of 'open letter'; in the Biblical context it would be sent by an apostle, such as Paul, for the instruction of the churches that believed Jesus Christ was the Messiah. However, some of Paul's letters are clearly private, such as those to Timothy, Titus and Philemon.

Foreknowledge – this obviously means 'to know in advance', but I mention it here because some people mix it up with predestination. Knowing in advance what is going to happen is not the same thing as prearranging every event.

Gentiles – every person who is not a Jew.

Jews - Because of Abraham's unparalleled faith, God promised him that his descendants were to be a great nation, a special people who would take God's message to the world. This unique nation have become known as the Jews. (They are also referred to as Israelites or the Children of Israel, the name the Lord gave to Jacob, Abraham's grandson). The name "Jew" is derived from the word Judah, who was one of Jacob's twelve sons. Originally its application was limited to his descendants, the tribe of Judah, but later came to apply to any one of the twelve tribes without distinction.

Law of Moses – a complicated set of very strict rules governing all aspects of life, which was given by God, through Moses, to the Jews. These Laws had to be adhered to if they were to become the special nation God wanted them to be.

Messiah – a Hebrew word that means 'The Anointed One', the one who was to, and indeed will, lead the Jews in a glorious future time when the whole nation would be obedient to God's wishes. 'Christ' is the Greek word for 'Messiah'.

Pentecost – a Jewish feast. It is described mainly in Leviticus 23:15-21 and Deuteronomy 16:9,10, where it is also called the Feast of Weeks.

Prayer – the dictionary definition is that prayer is 'a personal communication with a deity'. As Christians we believe we can communicate personally, by prayer, with God, Our Heavenly Father. To do this we must recognise that we need a mediator, a go-between if you like, and that this is 'the man Christ Jesus' (see 1 Timothy 2:5). Also see the references to further reading below.

Proselyte – a Gentile who wished to adopt the Jewish faith could become a proselyte. He would undergo a series of rituals, including circumcision, and take up the Jews' strict way of life with regard to the Law, including observance of the Sabbath.

Right Division – a method of studying the Scriptures which helps to define which parts of it are directly written to us, and what is the significance of the other parts.

Acknowledgements and Further Reading

A Light to my Path

Acknowledgements and Further Reading

This study was inspired by an old leaflet entitled 'Dispensational Truth' which we found among my mother's papers and which was written by A.J. Harrop. I've borrowed the phraseology here and there, hoping the author would not mind.

In this booklet, *A Light unto my Path,* I have tried to give a very brief introduction to Bible Study. Much has been left out, but I'm hoping you'll be encouraged to take the matter further and find out for yourself. If you're a complete beginner, my own personal advice would be to select a group, or a teacher, and stick with them for a while until you start to get a handle on the Scriptures. This is because there is so much to learn and just finding a place to start can be daunting. Never lose sight of the object of the exercise: to form your own conclusions by reference to the Scriptures, but accept that, at first, it can be a great thing to have someone show you around.

However, it is important to have a 'Berean' attitude. This word comes in Acts 17:6 and refers to a town in Macedonia, or northern Greece, called Berea. The people there, in their response to the Apostle Paul's preaching, stood out in two ways. First, they were eager to hear his teaching, and second, they studied the Scriptures every day to make certain that what they'd heard was true.

Studying the Scriptures daily is a very good habit to get into. Even if you're not sure what some of it means, it will give you a familiarity that will be invaluable to you, and often understanding comes later. For that reason the first item on my reading list is:

The Bible

No one's interpretation, however eloquent or convincing, can replace reading the real thing. Of course, most of us can't do that. We have to make do with a translation. In this booklet I've used mainly the *New International Version*, but these days there are lots of others. Try to find one you feel comfortable reading. Also be aware that as well as studying the scriptures, prayer and meditation have a part to play in deepening your understanding as well. My personal experience has been that this only works properly when you begin to be familiar with the text. It seems that God prefers not to do it all on His own; you have to give Him something to work with.

More on the Maze

More on the Maze

Helpful Books

For the beginner and anyone for whom right division is a new idea.

How to Approach the Bible
by Michael Penny

This books encourages the
reader to ask such questions as:

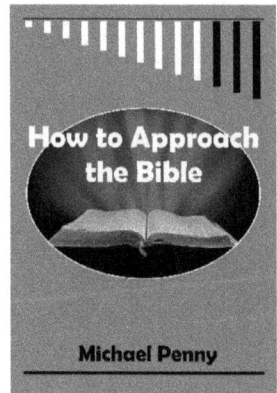

- WHO is the passages sent to?
- WHO is the passage about?
- WHERE is it about?
- WHEN was it written?
- WHEN is it about?

Asking such questions quickly leads to a better understanding.

Further details of the book opposite, and those on the following pages, can be seen on

www.obt.org.uk

All the books can be ordered from that website and also from

The Open Bible Trust,
Fordland Mount, Upper Basildon,
Reading, RG8 8LU, UK.

They are also available
as eBooks from Amazon and Apple
and as KDP paperbacks from Amazon.

Introducing the Books of the Bible
by Brian Sherring

This little book gives a good overview of the Bible for anyone whose Biblical knowledge is limited. It contains a brief description of what each of the books is about, and their relationship to each other and to God's overall plan.

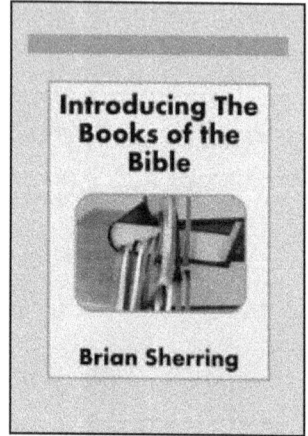

Introducing God's Plan
by Michael and Sylvia Penny

This also gives an overall perspective of the Bible, but in simpler language than Brian Sherring's book, and is recommended for anyone hoping to introduce the Scriptures to children, or for anyone older who has little or no knowledge of the Bible.

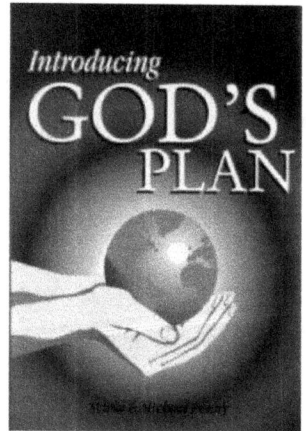

The Dividing Line: Acts 28
by David Tavender

This covers the subject matter of
'*A Light unto my Path*' and takes
it to the next stage.

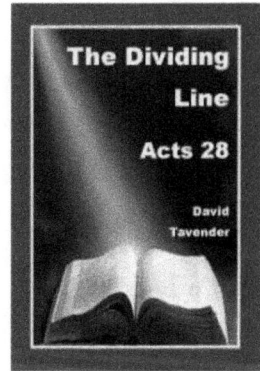

The Church! When Did it Begin?
(And why is that important?)
by Olive and Lloyd Allen

This is an excellent book, being
not only informative but very
readable. It also briefly covers
fundamental subjects such as how
the Bible came into being, and
considers several other frequently asked questions
which might not at first sight seem to be related to
right division.

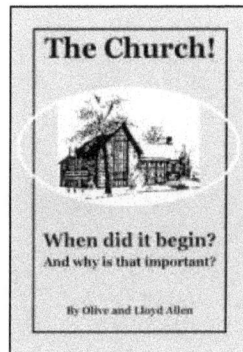

Prayer

I suggested earlier that prayer and meditation can help with understanding. However, many people seem to find prayer difficult, and often have a misconception about what prayer is for. Right division can help with this too. Also my experience has been that it's always hard to connect to someone, anyone, with whom you have nothing in common. Once you decide to take the plunge and begin working with the Lord, then you'll have something to talk about and it becomes a whole lot easier.

The Place of Prayer in an Age of Grace
by Michael Penny

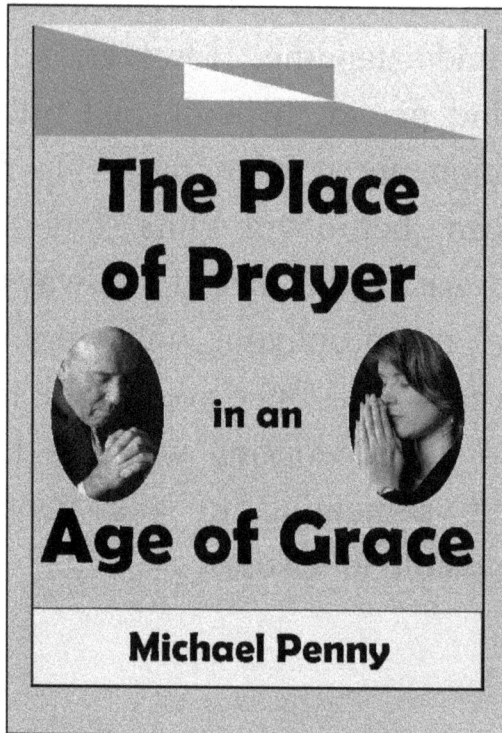

This publication emphasises that there was a change of dispensation which began at the end of the Acts of Apostles, and that the change of rules also encompasses prayer. Therefore, we need to base *our* prayer expectations on the parts of Scripture written after that time.

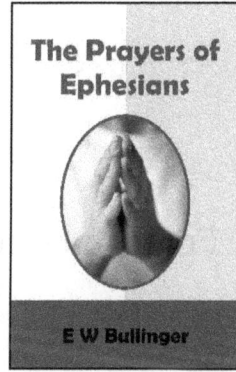

Unanswered Prayer
by Neville Stephens

Prayer that is Powerful and Effective
by Andrew Morton

The Prayers of Ephesians
by E W Bullinger

For further information about the books on the previous please visit

www.obt.org.uk

They can be ordered from that website and also from

The Open Bible Trust,
Fordland Mount, Upper Basildon,
Reading RG8 8LU, UK.

They are also available as
eBooks from Amazon and Apple
and also as KDP paperbacks from Amazon.

About the author

Eliza Wright was born in Sheffield in 1948 and was educated at Ecclesfield Grammar School. After leaving school she eventually began working at the mental hospital for the area, and qualified as a psychiatric nurse in 1976. A few years later her own health declined, dictating a less physically demanding life-style, and she chose further education.

After obtaining a BSc and PhD in chemistry from Sheffield University, she became a teacher and discovered that teaching was a far more arduous job than nursing. But to compensate for this she met her future husband there. In 1986 she and her husband left teaching and started their own business.

In 1994 they moved to the Isle of Skye where they still reside and are still self-employed in various computer-related areas. Despite her science background, she discovered an unexpected talent for embroidery design. Creating and publishing needlework projects based on the culture and scenery of the Scottish Islands is now her main occupation.

Also by Eliza Wright

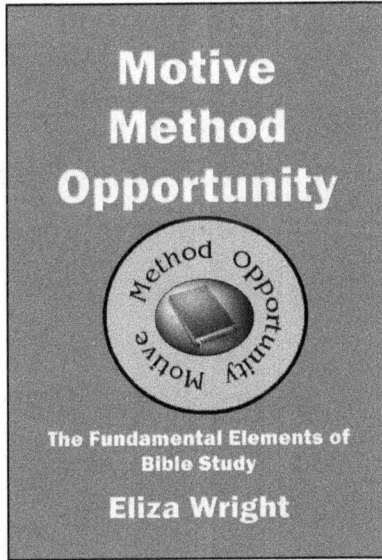

Motive
Method
Opportunity

The Fundamental Elements of
Bible Study

Eliza Wright

This book attempts to confront the following question: "Why, when Christians today have better access to information than at any time in history, do so many seem to be turning away from serious Bible Study?"

· Is this because they feel it has nothing to offer?
· Or because they do not know how to go about it?
· Or is it because they simply do not have time?

This book, however, is for those who already have some familiarity with the Scriptures, and who would like to take it further, but find themselves confronted by obstacles that they do not know how to overcome.

What the author suggests is an approach that might kindle a spark of genuine enthusiasm for discovery, and that this motivation may then lead to a more individual method for working out what is going on between the covers of the Book that many love to read but relatively few seem to study

Further reading

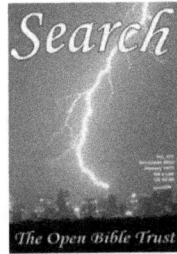

For a free sample of
The Open Bible Trust's magazine Search,
please visit

www.obt.org.uk/search

or email

admin@obt.org.uk

About this book

A Light unto my Path

There's a maze on the front cover of this booklet. A maze does not have just one path but a whole tangle of them, and for many people the Bible is a bit like a maze. It is a book where it is difficult to find one's way, and many get easily lost.

However, some people have a system for finding their way through a maze and this booklet demonstrates a system—right division—which shows the reader a path through the Bible.

Publications of The Open Bible Trust must be in accordance with its evangelical, fundamental and dispensational basis. However, beyond this minimum, writers are free to express whatever beliefs they may have as their own understanding, provided that the aim in so doing is to further the object of The Open Bible Trust.

A copy of the doctrinal basis is available at

www.obt.org.uk/doctrinal-basis

or from:

THE OPEN BIBLE TRUST
Fordland Mount, Upper Basildon,
Reading, RG8 8LU, UK.

www.ingramcontent.com/pod-product-compliance
Lightning Source LLC
Chambersburg PA
CBHW070535030426
42337CB00016B/2217